A Word About
Soccer

By Lynne Gibbs   Illustrated by Jan Smith

ISBN 0-7696-3386-2

50395

School Specialty
Publishing

First published in Great Britain in 2005 by Brimax
Publishing Ltd, Appledram Barns, Chichester PO20 7EQ
Copyright © 2005 Brimax Publishing Ltd
This edition published in 2005 by Brighter Child®, an
imprint of School Specialty Publishing, a member of the
School Specialty Family. Printed in China.

Columbus, Ohio

Library of Congress Cataloging-in-Publication
Data is on file with the publisher.

Send all inquiries to:
School Specialty Publishing
8720 Orion Place
Columbus, OH 43240-2111

ISBN 0-7696-3386-2

2 3 4 5 6 7 8 9 10 BRI 10 09 08 07 06

Soccer Fun

Soccer is one of the most popular sports that children play today.

It is great exercise because it involves running, kicking, and moving quickly.

3

What to Wear

Every soccer team has its own uniform.
The color and style identifies a team on the field.

shorts

long-sleeved shirt

short-sleeved shirt

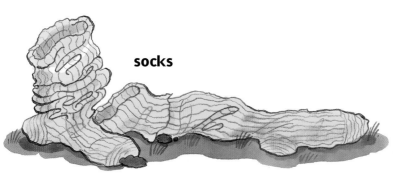

socks

Types of shoes

cleats

Modern soccer shoes are flexible. Some shoes have cleats on their bottoms. These shoes are most suitable for dry field conditions.

interchangeable cleats

Some shoes have screw-in cleats. This means that they can be changed to suit the ground conditions: hard, soft, or wet and slippery.

artificial turf

When playing on artificial turf, shoes with textured bottoms work well. These shoes give a better grip on hard surfaces and also cushion the feet.

shin guards

To protect your legs, you should wear shin guards. These are worn under your socks.

Playing as a Team

In soccer, every player has an important job to do.

Who's on a Soccer Team?

Soccer is a team sport where players try to score goals by passing and dribbling a ball across a field, and then kicking or heading it into the opposing team's goal. Except for the goalkeeper and when players take throw-ins, players are not allowed to touch the ball with their hands or arms. There are eleven players on a soccer team.

Positions

goalkeeper

Also called a "goalie" or "keeper," a goalkeeper has to stop opponents from putting the ball into the goal. The goalkeeper is the only player allowed to use the hands when handling the ball.

forward

A forward's job is to put the ball into the back of the net. A good forward has to have the speed and coordination to move away from the opponents and score.

midfield player

When attacking, midfield players move the ball up the field and try to pass it to a team member who can score.

defender

A defender's main job is to prevent the other team's players from having a chance to score. They do this by guarding attacking players and putting them under pressure.

Developing Soccer Skills

Good soccer skills are developed through practice. Practice can take place anywhere—on a regulation soccer field, in a park, or in a backyard.

Soccer Skills

Controlling the ball is the most important skill to learn in soccer. Players also must be able to perform trick shots or moves to surprise their opponents.

Kicks and Passes

chest pass

Soccer players can use their chests to redirect a ball to another player by quickly turning left or right.

header

A header can be used to shoot or deflect the ball with one's head.

back heel pass

A back heel pass can be made with the heel or the sole of the foot to a trailing teammate.

overhead kick

1. When the ball is about head high, the player takes off on one leg, jumping backwards.

2. Keeping the eyes on the ball, the player swings the kicking foot up over the head.

3. At the highest part of the jump, the player strikes the ball.

13

The Soccer Field

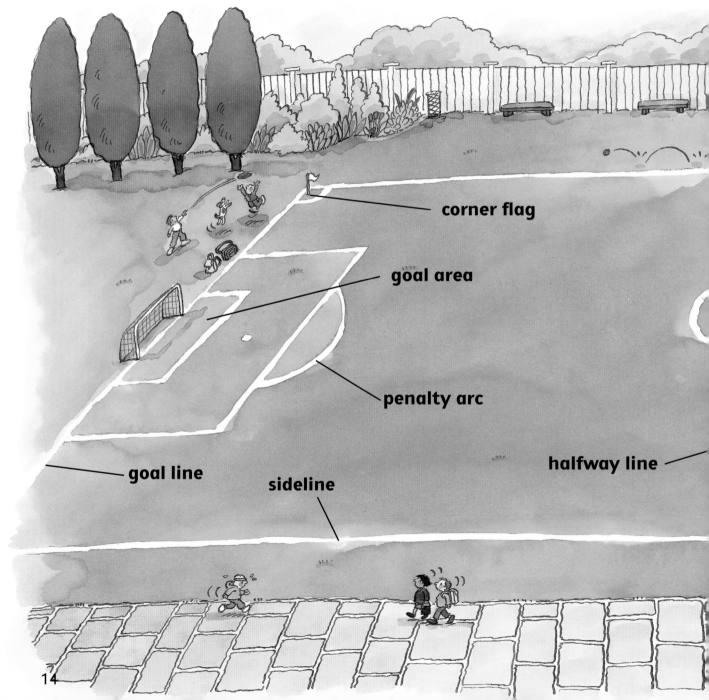

corner flag

goal area

penalty arc

goal line

sideline

halfway line

A regulation soccer field is rectangular and ranges from 100 to 130 yards long and 50 to 100 yards wide. The parts of a soccer field are labeled below.

center mark

corner arc

penalty area

center circle

penalty spot

goal

15

On the Field

White paint is used to mark the different areas of the field.

center mark

The center mark designates the center of the field. It is the point where the game starts.

sideline

A throw-in takes place when the ball crosses the sideline. The throw is taken from the spot where the ball crossed the line and by the team who did not put the ball out of play.

penalty spot

The ball is placed on the penalty spot for a penalty kick. A penalty can be given if the defending team fouls in their own penalty area. When a penalty is being taken, all the other players must stand outside the penalty area until the ball is kicked.

corner arc

A corner kick is awarded when the ball crosses the goal line and was last touched by a member of the defending team.

Field Formations

A formation is the basic shape of a soccer team on the field. Each team can arrange its defenders, midfield, and attacking players in a variety of ways.

four-four-two

4-3-3 is an attack formation. The three forwards spread across the field to attack the goal.

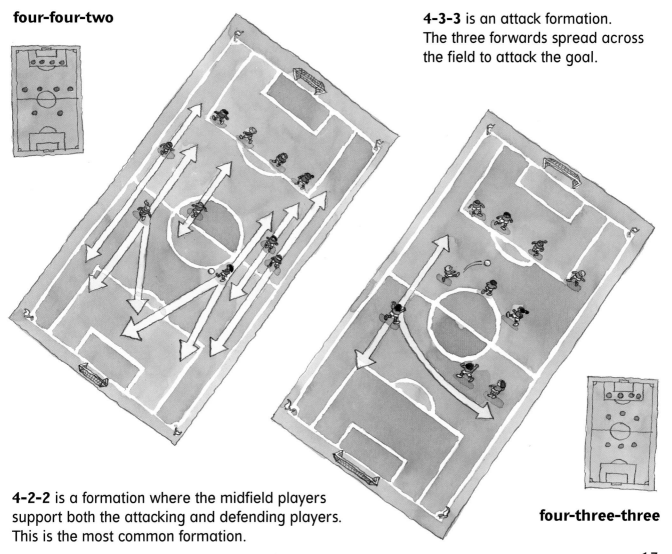

4-2-2 is a formation where the midfield players support both the attacking and defending players. This is the most common formation.

four-three-three

An Official Soccer Match

In an official soccer match, there is an official or referee who makes sure that the team follows the rules. The official also ensures that the team members and fans practice good sportsmanship.

Blowing the Whistle

There are many strict rules to follow in professional soccer. The referee is on the field to make sure the players on each team obey the rules during a match.

Rules

whistle

The referee starts and stops play by blowing a whistle.

referee

free kick

The referee awards a free kick to the opposing team when a foul is committed outside the penalty area.

yellow card

The referee holds up a yellow card to show when a player has been warned.

red card

The referee uses a red card when a player has been asked to leave the field.

offside rule

The referee also blows a whistle when a player is offside. A player is offside if he or she is closer to the opponent's goal line than the ball at the moment it is passed to that player, unless there are two or more opposition players at least as close to their goal line.

linesmen

To assist the referee, two linesmen watch the game from opposite sides of the field.

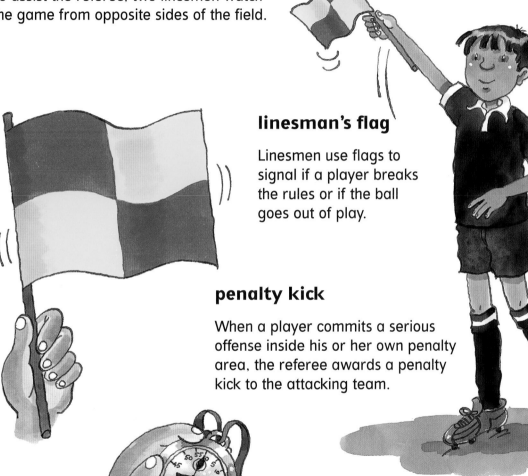

linesman's flag

Linesmen use flags to signal if a player breaks the rules or if the ball goes out of play.

penalty kick

When a player commits a serious offense inside his or her own penalty area, the referee awards a penalty kick to the attacking team.

keeping time

A match consists of two halves of 45 minutes each. The referee can add extra time if the game has been delayed by injury.

Practicing at Home

Every soccer player needs to practice certain skills. Here are some exercises recommended by the top players and coaches to help improve ball control and fitness.

Keeping the ball in the air

The goal of this exercise is to keep the ball in the air for as long as possible without letting it touch the ground. You can use your feet, your thighs, or your head to control the ball and keep it in the air. You can also bounce the ball alternately on your head and foot.

Don't forget to warm up before you begin any exercises. Swing your arms, twist your hips, and jog in place.

Once you can control the ball with your feet, thighs, and head, try combining all the exercises—foot, thigh, head, thigh, foot.

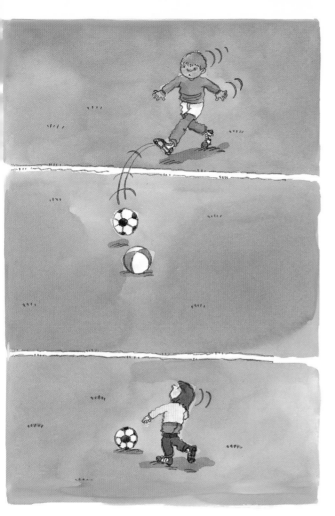

Follow the leader

This exercise is for two or more players. Choose one person to be the leader. This person dribbles the ball. Players line up behind the leader and follow every move he or she makes. The leader must make lots of turns, stops, and changes of speed. After a minute, the leader must pass the ball backwards and join the back of the line. Then, the next player becomes the leader, and so on, until all the players have had a chance to be the leader.

Target practice

This exercise is for two players. Divide an area in three equal parts, or "thirds." The two players face each other in the two "thirds" that are furthest apart. Each player has a ball. A brightly colored ball, the target, is placed in the center of the middle "third." Players must try to move this target across the other player's line and into their area by striking it with their own ball.

Glossary

back heel pass Made with the heel or sole of the foot to a trailing teammate.

center mark Designates the center of the field and is the point where the game starts.

chest pass Used to redirect the ball to another player by quickly turning left or right.

cleats Often used on the bottoms of soccer shoes; most suitable for dry conditions.

corner kick This kick is awarded when the ball crosses the goal line and was last touched by a member of the defending team.

dribbling A way for players to move the ball up the field, keeping it close to their feet as they run.

formation The basic shape of a soccer team on the field.

forward This player's job is to put the ball into the back of the net.

free kick Given to the opposition when a foul is committed outside the penalty area.

goal A net structure at either end of the field, used to kick the soccer ball in to score a goal.

goalkeeper Member of a soccer team who guards his or her team's goal.

header A shot from the head, used to shoot or deflect the ball.

interchangeable cleats Cleats that can be changed to adapt to different ground conditions—hard, soft, or wet and slippery.

linesman's flag Used when a player breaks the rules or if the ball goes out of play.

linesmen To assist the referee, two linesmen watch the game from opposite sides of the field.

match A soccer game.

midfield player Moves the ball up the field and tries to pass to a team member who can score.

official match Two halves of 45 minutes each.

offside When a player is closer to the opponent's goal line than the ball at the moment it is passed to that player.

overhead kick When a player swings the kicking foot up over the head and strikes the ball.

penalty When a player commits a serious offense inside his or her own penalty area, the referee awards the attacking team a penalty kick.

red card Held up by the referee to show that a player has been asked to leave the field.

referee An official who controls a soccer match and makes the decision when to stop and restart play.

shin guards Worn under socks to protect the legs.

team The eleven members needed on each side to play in a match.

throw-in Takes place when the ball crosses the sideline. The throw is taken from the spot where the ball crossed the line and by the team who did not put the ball out of play.

yellow card Held up by the referee to show that a player has been warned.